SPOTLIGHT ON AMERICAN HISTORY

The Gold Rush
Gold Seekers, Miners, and Merchants

Mina Flores

PowerKiDS press™

New York

Published in 2017 by The Rosen Publishing Group, Inc.
29 East 21st Street, New York, NY 10010

Book Design: Tanya Dellaccio

Photo Credits: Cover Stock Montage/Archive Photo/Getty Images; p. 4 https://commons.wikimedia.org/wiki/File:JohannAugustSutter.jpg; p. 5 https://commons.wikimedia.org/wiki/File:Sutters_Mill.jpg; p. 6 https://commons.wikimedia.org/wiki/File:SpanishMissionsinCA.png; pp. 7, 12, 15, 19 Everett Historical/Shutterstock.com; p. 9 American School/Getty Images; p. 10 https://commons.wikimedia.org/wiki/File:SanFranciscoharbor1851c_sharp.jpg; p. 11 https://commons.wikimedia.org/wiki/File:California_Clipper_500.jpg; p. 13 https://commons.wikimedia.org/wiki/File:California_Gold_Diggers.jpg; p. 14 General Photographic Agency / Stringer/Hulton Archive/Getty Images; p. 17 courtesy of Library Of Congress; p. 18 https://commons.wikimedia.org/wiki/File:Chinese_Emigration_to_America.jpg; p. 21 Print Collector/Contributor/Hulton Archive/Getty Images.

Library of Congress Cataloging-in-Publication Data

Names: Flores, Mina, author.
Title: The Gold Rush : gold seekers, miners, and merchants / Mina Flores.
Description: New York : PowerKids Press, 2016. | Series: Spotlight on American history | Includes index.
Identifiers: LCCN 2015049082 | ISBN 9781508149569 (pbk.) | ISBN 9781508149422 (library bound) | ISBN 9781508149217 (6 pack)
Subjects: LCSH: California--Gold discoveries--Juvenile literature. | California--History--1846-1850--Juvenile literature. | Frontier and pioneer life--California--Juvenile literature.
Classification: LCC F865 .F64 2016 | DDC 979.4/03--dc23
LC record available at http://lccn.loc.gov/2015049082

Manufactured in the United States of America

CPSIA Compliance Information: Batch #BS16PK: For further information contact Rosen Publishing, New York, New York at 1-800-237-9932.

CONTENTS

GOLD! 4

OWNING THE WEST 6

AMERICA'S DESTINY 8

GETTING TO CALIFORNIA 10

GOLD FEVER 12

LIFE AS A MINER 14

BOOMTOWNS AND CITIES 16

SEEKING *GAM SAAN* 18

HOSTILITY 20

A GOLDEN LEGACY 22

GLOSSARY 23

INDEX 24

PRIMARY SOURCE LIST 24

WEBSITES 24

GOLD!

In 1839, a German **immigrant** named John Sutter arrived in the territory that later became the state of California. He helped found a settlement called New Helvetia. Within a few years, he built a large fort, successfully farmed acres of land, and owned thousands of cattle. However, the most memorable event of Sutter's business in California happened in 1848.

John Sutter

A man poses in front of Sutter's sawmill, close to where James Marshall discovered gold.

In January of that year, Sutter had a crew of men build a sawmill along the American River, near Coloma. On January 24, a carpenter named James Marshall looked into the riverbed and saw nuggets of gold! Sutter tried to keep the discovery a secret, but word soon got out, and the California gold rush began. By 1849, more than 80,000 people had come to California in search of fortune. Who were the gold seekers, miners, and merchants who flocked to this territory, and how did they shape this **era** of history?

OWNING THE WEST

California wasn't always part of the United States. The territory was claimed by Spain in 1542. Spain also owned Mexico. In 1821, Mexico won its independence from Spain. Mexico took control of the **missions** and pueblos, or towns, that were established in California when it was under Spain's rule. American settlers began arriving in California territory around this time.

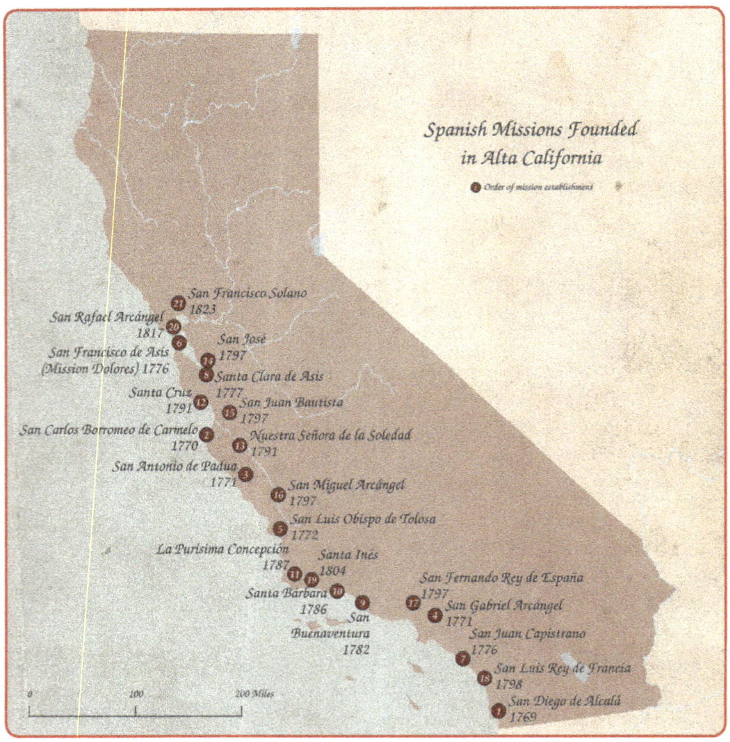

This map shows the location of missions in California in 1821. A route called "El Camino Real" connected them.

Fighting in California ended in 1847, but continued in other places until 1848.

California's coast became a spot for trade, and fur trappers and traders created land routes into the territory. Though the number of American settlers was growing, they were under Mexican rule. Soon, they desired to break away from it.

In May 1846, war broke out between Mexico and the United States over where the border was between the countries. Americans in Sonoma, California, revolted against Mexican rule and joined the United States in war. The U.S.-Mexican War ended in 1848 with the signing of the Treaty of Guadalupe Hidalgo. The treaty gave the United States ownership of California.

AMERICA'S DESTINY

California's population grew quickly after gold was discovered. People who traveled to California to hunt for gold were called '49ers, as many arrived in 1849.

Historians say the gold rush was one of the largest **migrations** in U.S. history. The gold rush occurred during a period known as westward **expansion**. This was a time when many Americans moved to unsettled western territories.

Westward expansion was encouraged by an idea called Manifest Destiny. This was the belief that it was the United States' duty to stretch west to the Pacific Ocean.

Americans had plenty of land to choose from as they moved west. The United States gained great amounts of land through the Louisiana Purchase in 1803. Beginning in the 1830s, pioneers traveled in covered wagons and started settling the **frontier**. To many, the West represented freedom and a chance for a new beginning. It also presented economic opportunities—especially after people learned there was gold there.

'49ers mine for gold in the Calaveras River, hoping to find a fortune in its waters.

GETTING TO CALIFORNIA

There were two routes to California from the East. Some people traveled the Oregon-California Trail in covered wagons. The journey was long and difficult. On average, it took about six months. Wagons traveled through rough, unsettled land, some of which was occupied by Native American groups. They weren't always friendly to settlers passing through their homelands.

San Francisco grew rapidly as gold seekers arrived through its ports. The buildings and homes seen here were just a few years old when this photograph was taken in 1850 or 1851.

This sailing card advertised a ship that sailed from Boston to San Francisco. It promises a "very quick trip" to the other side of the country.

Settlers could also travel by sea. Ships sailed from the East Coast, around the tip of South America, to San Diego or San Francisco. This voyage took six months, too, and many passengers experienced sickness and poor conditions on the ships. When the Panama Railway was completed, it offered a faster and more direct route to California.

Americans weren't the only people journeying long distances for gold. Gold seekers also came from other countries, including China, Germany, France, Ireland, Mexico, and Turkey. With gold seekers pouring in from all over the world, California's population became very **diverse**.

GOLD FEVER

You might think Americans were very excited to learn of gold in California. Not at first! When a newspaper called the *Californian* reported the discovery in 1848, people in San Francisco didn't really believe it. A couple of weeks later, local papers reported that the news didn't excite people.

Because the news wasn't widely believed, it took a little while for Americans to seize the

Most gold seekers were men. Many left their families behind to seek fortune in California.

People of all backgrounds, from all over the world, came to find gold in California's rivers.

golden opportunity. People from other countries got a head start on them. The first boat carrying Chinese workers arrived in California in February 1848.

Gold fever among Californians began in May 1848. A man named Sam Brannan is said to have started it. Brannan owned a store near Sutter's Fort, and he received gold dust as payment from a customer. He then went to the streets, shouting, "Gold! Gold! Gold from the American River!" Within weeks, Californians had abandoned their jobs and their towns as they rushed to the rivers to find gold.

LIFE AS A MINER

Gold seekers got straight to work once they arrived in California. Miners set up camp by streams and rivers, which are where they searched for gold. Tents belonging to gold seekers dotted the riverbanks.

Miners quickly discovered that mining for gold was hard labor. Using just metal pans, shovels, and picks, they worked in all kinds of weather, digging up dirt and moving rocks. They spent

A simple shovel and pan were all some miners needed to find gold.

In this illustration, miners use a sluice to search for gold. A sluice is a tool that controls the flow of water.

time in freezing steams and rivers. Many miners fell ill, and some even lost fingernails from the work!

The first miners tried to find gold using a method called panning. They placed gravel and water from a stream into a pan and shook it back and forth. The heavy gold sank to the bottom of the pan, while the lighter matter stayed toward the top. More **complex** methods were used to mine gold from the mountains, which was even harder.

BOOMTOWNS AND CITIES

As people poured into California, boomtowns began appearing all over the state. A boomtown is a settlement that grows quickly because of an important discovery nearby. Hangtown, Sucker Flat, and Murderer's Bar were just some of the mining towns that sprang up in California during this time.

The population growth presented opportunities to more than just gold seekers. **Enterprising** people found they could make money by setting up stores, **saloons**, banks, and theaters. San Francisco, at the center of the activity, experienced major economic growth. Many shop owners benefitted from selling goods and services to miners. For example, Sam Brannan made $36,000 from selling goods in the summer of 1848.

This growth continued even after the gold rush ended. Many Chinese immigrants became business owners when they opened laundry services and restaurants. Soon, San Francisco's Chinatown neighborhood was a **thriving** center of business.

San Francisco was a busy city by the time this drawing was created in 1851. Today, it's one of the largest cities in the United States.

SEEKING *GAM SAAN*

People of many backgrounds were drawn to California, but Chinese immigrants, especially, came in large numbers. The United States' Chinese population was small before the gold rush. By 1851, about 25,000 Chinese people had come to California to find their fortune.

Some Chinese immigrants came to America to escape a life of poverty in China. Many people in

Chinese immigrants sailed to America on small, crowded ships.

Chinese miners settled in mining camps along California's rivers.

China depended on farming to make a living, but high taxes from a war with Britain caused many farmers and peasants to lose their land. When the news of gold reached China, people sent their sons to America, hoping they could send money back to China to help their families.

Chinese gold seekers traveled to America by ship. They set sail from the port city of Guangzhou and arrived in San Francisco after an eight-week journey. They hoped to find wealth at *Gam Saan*, which are the Cantonese words for "Gold Mountain."

HOSTILITY

Mexicans also came to California in large numbers. About 2,000 Mexican miners were in California in 1848, and by 1849, that number had risen to 6,000. Native Americans and African Americans were counted among gold seekers, too. These groups experienced **hostility**. In fact, hostility toward nonwhite miners was common in mining camps and towns.

As more people arrived in California, competition increased and gold became harder to find. Some American miners felt they deserved gold more than people from other countries. White miners' anger caused them to **discriminate** against people of other races, and these feelings sometimes led to violence.

In 1850, California lawmakers passed the Foreign Miners Tax, which charged foreign miners a fee of $20 a month. The tax caused many Chinese gold seekers to give up on mining, and they were forced to find other jobs.

When mining became too expensive or too competitive, Chinese immigrants turned to business. Chinese men are shown here, shopping in a San Francisco marketplace.

A GOLDEN LEGACY

The gold rush affected California in many ways. Its population had grown so quickly that the territory became a state in 1850, just two years after gold was discovered.

San Francisco became one of the fastest-growing cities in the world because of the gold rush. The hundreds of thousands of people arriving in the area passed through the city, and many stuck around to set up shops and businesses that turned San Francisco into a booming economic center.

The gold rush also affected California's culture, as it brought people from many backgrounds to the state. However, tensions between Americans and foreigners, as well as between whites and nonwhites, resulted in discrimination and violence. California's economy suffered in the 1870s and many felt the Chinese immigrants were taking away Americans' jobs. In 1882, Congress passed the Chinese Exclusion Act, which banned immigration from China until 1943.

Though California's gold rush only lasted a short time, its impact on the area—as well as the United States—was enormous.

GLOSSARY

complex (kahm-PLEKS): Having many parts.

discriminate (dis-KRIH-muh-nayt): To treat someone or a group of people unfairly.

diverse (dy-VURHS): Made of many different cultures.

enterprising (EHN-tuhr-pry-zing): Showing a willingness to find opportunities.

era (AIR-uh): A period of time.

expansion (ihk-SPAN-shun): The act of getting larger or spreading out.

frontier (fruhn-TEER): The limit of settled land, beyond which lies unsettled territory.

hostility (hah-STIH-luh-tee): Anger.

immigrant (IH-muh-grunt): Somebody who comes to live in another country.

migration (my-GRAY-shun): Movement from one place to another.

mission (MIH-shuhn): Religious settlements set up by missionaries, who are people who work to spread their religion.

saloon (suh-LOON): A bar.

thriving (THRY-ving): Successful, strong.

INDEX

A

American River, 5, 13

B

Brannan, Sam, 13, 16

C

California, 4, 5, 6, 7, 8, 10, 11, 12, 13, 14, 16, 18, 19, 20, 22

China, 11, 18, 19, 22

Chinatown, 16

Chinese Exclusion Act, 22

F

Foreign Miners Tax, 20

G

Gam Saan, 19

H

Hangtown, 16

L

Louisiana Purchase, 8

M

Manifest Destiny, 8

Marshall, James, 5

Mexico, 6, 7, 11

Murderer's Bar, 16

O

Oregon-California Trail, 10

P

Panama Railway, 11

N

New Helvetia, 4

S

San Diego, 11

San Francisco, 10, 11, 12, 16, 17, 19, 21, 22

Spain, 6

Sucker Flat, 16

Sutter, John, 4, 5, 13

T

Treaty of Guadalupe Hidalgo, 7

U

U.S.-Mexican War, 7

PRIMARY SOURCE LIST

Page 4: *Johann August Sutter*. Created by Frank Buchser. Oil on canvas. 1866. Now kept in the Kunstmuseum Solothurn, Solothurn, Switzerland.

Page 5: Sutter's sawmill. Created by R.H. Vance. Photomechanical reproduction of a daguerreotype. ca. 1850. Now kept in the Library of Congress Prints and Photographs Division, Washington, D.C.

Page 10: View of San Francisco harbor. Created by Sterling C. McIntyre. Half-plate daguerreotype. January 1851. Now kept in the Library of Congress Prints and Photographs Division, Washington, D.C.

Page 18: *Chinese emigration to America: sketch on board the steamship Alaska, bound for San Francisco.* Published in *The Graphic* and *Harper's Weekly*. April 29, 1876. Now kept at the Bancroft Library at the University of California, Berkeley, Berkeley, California.

WEBSITES

Due to the changing nature of Internet links, PowerKids Press has developed an online list of websites related to the subject of this book. This site is updated regularly. Please use this link to access the list: www.powerkidslinks.com/soah/gold